LOST IN
ICELAND

with Sigurgeir Sigurjónsson

Forlagið

Special thanks to:

Helga Gísladóttir, John Gústafsson, Anna María Sigurjónsdóttir, Unnur Jökulsdóttir, Gunnar Örn Gunnarsson, Þröstur Magnússon and Ragnar Tómasson.

PRONUNCIATION NOTE
The Icelandic letter þ (capital Þ) is pronounced like the English *th* in "think", and the letter ð (capital Ð) like the *th* in "then".

LOST IN ICELAND © Sigurgeir Sigurjónsson 2002
Photographs © Sigurgeir Sigurjónsson 2002
Text © Forlagið 2002
Preface: Guðmundur Andri Thorsson
Translation of preface: Bernard Scudder
Additional text: Victoria Cribb
Design and layout: Klingenberg & Cochran/Elísabet A. Cochran
Page layout: Eyjólfur Jónsson
Printing: Prentmiðlun/China

Forlagið · Reykjavík · 2013

First edition 2002
Second edition 2013

ISBN 978-9979-53-582-9

www.forlagid.is

CONTENTS

Driftwood and angelica line the shore of Hornvík bay in the uninhabited Hornstrandir region, nortwest Iceland.

Basalt columns form an architectural display at the Litlanesfoss falls in the Hengifossá river, Fljótsdalur, east Iceland.

Guðmundur Andri Thorsson

IS THERE A SPIRIT IN THE MOUNTAIN?

Conflicting feelings do battle in the mind of any Icelander who is confronted by photographs of his country's nature: veneration, fear, devotion, helplessness, pride. All these feelings come to the fore when Icelanders discuss how the land should be treated. What on earth are we supposed to do with all that water? All those mountains, all that wind, all that wilderness? Or should we perhaps do nothing? Iceland is one of the last countries in Europe where, in spite of modernization, nature reigns independent – in other words, where nature appears to have a will independent of man, a will that people have not managed to subjugate after centuries of trying. The history of Iceland up to the 20th century is the story of successive defeats by the raging elements, when volcanoes destroyed farms and farmland, felling livestock and pushing people to the brink of starvation. It was not until the advent of 20th-century technology – geothermal space heating, concrete, insulated housing, trawlers, four-wheel drives, not forgetting the "tussock flattener" for levelling out fields – that Iceland became fit to live in, awoke from centuries of dormancy. Such dynamic energy was released and such *joie de vivre* that Iceland's population became one of the richest in the world. They were like someone who has always been cold and, when he finally reaches the warmth, cannot control his joy.

Confronted by these photographs of Icelandic nature, the Icelander admires its beauty, but somewhere within him dwells the knowledge that nature could turn against him, could destroy him. He knows that nature almost exterminated his nation. This hard-earned wisdom about nature's basic instinct is preserved in the collective memory in a lullaby sung to all Icelandic children. It describes the black sand eradicating green pastures and the glacier where death-deep fissures resound – anyone who has heard a glacier creeping knows what terrifying sound the author is referring to.

~

In Iceland, the weather is referred to as "him". People say: "Now he's from the north," "he's calming down," etc. And "he" is always up to something. Sometimes "he" bursts forth in terrible gusts, sweeping everything that can be swept away out into the far beyond, and sometimes "he" is terribly kind and gentle: the same word, blíða, is used in Iceland for kindness and calm weather. "He" never rests; "he" is continually assaulting us from new directions and trying out ever-new types of weather. When I was a small boy visiting my grandfather, I had to sit and remain silent while grandfather listened to drawn-out accounts on the radio of what the weather had been like an hour before. I did not know then that my grandfather was keeping an eye on "him" the way some Icelanders still do, driven by an incurable gambler's passion, trying to predict "his" next trick – even with the aim of turning the tables on "him" for once. Who is he, anyway, this "he"? Of course it is the wind, personified under the name Kári, but it is also as if this figure of speech enshrines a deep-rooted attitude towards the whole of nature on the Icelanders' part: "he" is the worthy opponent. The eternal, faceless, cunning and deadly opponent.

~

Confronted with these photographs of Icelandic nature, you can almost hear them. Photographs of people are often frozen motion – the moment made eternal. In nature photography, the opposite applies. Here, instead of the moment being frozen and made eternal, eternity is frozen and made into a moment. We are granted a glimpse of eternity itself. A mountain doesn't wander much. And although water flows and water falls, that motion precisely recalls eternity – in flux. A profound tranquillity dwells in these photographs, and when you scrutinize them you soon begin to hear a profound silence. Some people claim that in the silence of Iceland's wilderness, you come closest to hearing God.

~

Icelanders are arguing now about whether the waterfalls in the highlands north of the Vatnajökull glacier ought to be harnessed or protected. Many subscribe to the 20th-century creed that we should subjugate this land with the technology that is finally at our disposal – the technology that has enabled us to live decent lives here – and finally take revenge, so to speak; take that tremendous force that once laid communities waste, and turn it to our material benefit. Others say they fail to see the benefit of using energy from waterfalls to drive factories, and describe hydropower projects as if they were sacrilegious – almost as if the plan were to harness God. Their standpoint towards nature is a religious one, typified by devotion and a longing to harness the awesome force inherent in Icelandic nature for the service of the human mind above all else; to go up into the mountains and perceive there some kind of force that is higher and mightier than man, to come into contact with that force and draw strength from it.

   This perspective may appear on first impression to be a romantic, 19th-century one, but it has deeper roots in the Icelandic consciousness than many advocates of hydropower would admit. From the earliest days of the settlement, a kind of animism has been endemic in Iceland, a belief in "sticks and stones", hidden people who live in rocks, trolls in the mountains, horses and cows in lakes, not to mention the complex groupings of all manner of ghosts which have always roamed the country. If there is any distinctively Icelandic branch of Christianity, it must lie in the strange admixture of ecclesiastical doctrine and these heathen notions, whereby belief in elves and hidden beings in nature still thrives alongside faith in Jesus the Saviour. Add to this the deep-rooted sense that the wilderness, the central highlands, are terra incognita, the *wilds*. When people had little idea about their land in centuries past, they spun yarns about the outlaws' flourishing hideaways in grassy valleys among the mountains, to say nothing of the land spirits that were supposed to inhabit them. Many people are wary of having much to do with such land – opening it too much, dashing away the veil of secrecy that still envelops the central highlands, to many people's minds. The central highlands are often seen to be where the country's heart beats.

~

Confronted with these photographs, alongside the feeling of profound silence, a suspicion arises that this silence is so absolute, so taut, so great and so profound, that it is not silence at all.

~

A woman from the West Fjords, where mountains tower over the villages and towns, never felt at home in Reykjavík because she found everything there so flat and characterless. A schoolboy from Akureyri, where the mountains are a reasonable distance away, could not stand living in the East Fjords, where he felt they were closing in on him. All these Icelanders, in turn, are unanimous that Denmark has a fairly nondescript landscape with no mountains, and none of them would dream of envying the Danes all their arable land. I do not know whether it suggests an animist streak, but the Icelanders talk about mountains the way Italians talk about football teams. They all support their own mountain. And people argue passionately which is more beautiful and remarkable, this mountain or that. In some of the sagas, people entered mountains at the end of their lives to become guardian spirits there, they became one with their mountain, while one of Halldór Laxness' best-loved novels, *The Light of the World*, ends with the main character walking onto the glacier where the land ceases to be earthly and merges with the heavens. In other words: nothing is more mundane than the mountain

11

you were brought up with, nothing is closer to you, yet that mountain is the sacred earth itself. It links you with eternity.

~

One thing above all others haunts Icelanders who are confronted by these photographs: where is that and what is it called? A photo of a mountain is never just a photo of a mountain, but a photo of a definite mountain with a specific name and shape and history. The people who settled Iceland in the ninth and tenth centuries, largely from Norway and the British Isles, were perhaps not particularly successful in conquering the land, except in one respect: they beset it with words, naming all the landmarks from mountain to shore, invariably associating them with a story of some kind. People created texts from the land. Every little hill in Iceland has a name of its own, every ridge, every mountain stream, and when an Icelander travels through his country, a large part of the journey involves reciting the names found on all sides. There's "Waterfall Hill"; there's "Unicorn"; look, there are the "Light Mountains". Why does he mutter away to himself like this? To bring the land close to him, to sense it as a part of himself. You may have never been there, but once you are told that a valley is named "Sudden Valley", you know the place, you have some kind of power over it. In *Songlines*, Bruce Chatwin recounts how the Australian aborigines travel through their country along invisible songlines which apparently exist in both the land and the people; how they sing the land as they go walkabout across it. In the same way, the Icelander chants his land, anoints it with lovely names that both illuminate the landscape and give it character. And above all else, by chanting these names you make contact with the spirits of your forebears who chanted these names too.

~

Besides their distinguishing national trait of talking more than anyone else about their national traits, the Icelanders differ from their neighbours in an important way – they are almost entirely at the mercy of nature. The factions squabbling about what to do with their waterfalls think along similar lines in regarding nature as the be-all and end-all of life in their country. It gives and it takes. It is the force that envelops life in Iceland and everyone yields to it in the end. "The king wants to sail but the breeze must prevail," runs an ancient saying that is often quoted to show how everything is at the mercy of nature. It is our mother and our enemy.

~

Is there a spirit in the mountain? Heathens believed so in the past, and Christians up to this day. Those who are raised beside a mountain carry that mountain inside them ever after – the mountain has made its home within them. And people's thoughts beneath a mountain gradually take their shape from the mountain. The mountain becomes an integral part of the lives of the people around it, and their thoughts about the mountain gradually become the mountain's spirit. But can the stones speak? Does a soul dwell in every flower? Is there a spirit in the mountain? Of course there is. And it is a whimsical spirit and it arouses conflicting feelings among the citizens of that land, leaving us sometimes fearful, sometimes full of veneration, devotion, helplessness, pride ...

Right: The spectacular Gullfoss (Golden Falls), in southwest Iceland,
is probably the most photographed waterfall in the country.

Idyllic view of the Skaftafell and Svínafell glacial tongues, with Hvannadalshnjúkur (2,110 m), Iceland's highest peak, to the right, southeast Iceland.

Birch woods thrive on the slopes of Svínafellsfjall,
in the lee of the Öræfajökull glacier, southeast Iceland.

Hofskirkja (1883–85), one of the last churches to be built
in the traditional turf style, Öræfi district, southeast Iceland.

A lone rowan tree marks the spot where the farm of Sandfell once stood, Öræfi district, southeast Iceland.

Icebergs calved from the Breiðamerkurjökull glacier float in the Jökulsárlón glacial lagoon, southeast Iceland.

Crossing the Núpsvötn river on the way to Núpsstaðarskógur,
near the Vatnajökull ice-cap, southeast Iceland.

The farmhouse at Hvalnes is dwarfed by Mt. Eystra-Horn,
Austur-Skaftafellssýsla district, southeast Iceland.

The black-grained snout of the Skeiðarárjökull glacier, the scene of devastating floods in 1996, Vatnajökull ice-cap, southeast Iceland.

Baulutjörn (Roaring Pond) and Fláajökull (Flaying Glacier) in southeast Iceland.
According to legend the water is haunted by a flayed bull.

Above: Hekla (1,491 m), in south Iceland, is one of the country's most active volcanoes, erupting at least 18 times since records began.

Right: Brúarfoss (Bridge Falls), also in the south, derives its name from a natural stone arch which once spanned the river.

Mýrdalsjökull is the country's southernmost ice-cap, and covers an area of around 595 km^2.

Family members attend the spring lambing at the farm
of Hvoll in Fljótshverfi district, southeast Iceland.

The aftermath of the spring shearing: the sheep will spend
the summer running wild in the mountains.

Above: Herding sheep during the autumn round-up,
near Baulutjörn pond, Fláajökull glacier beyond, southeast Iceland.

Right: Seljalandsfoss, one of Iceland's highest waterfalls,
plunges in a slender arc from the cliffs of the Eyjafjöll range, south Iceland.

Clouds above the black expanse of Mýrdalssandur, south Iceland.
Sandstorms can make driving in this desert a nerve-wracking business.

Skyscape over Lómagnúpur, southeast Iceland. The country's highest
mountain, Hvannadalshnjúkur (2,110 m), can be seen in the background.

Þingvellir national park in southwest Iceland, former meeting place of the Althing, one of the world's oldest parliaments.

Fissures in the lava at Þingvellir, in southwest Iceland, provide an eloquent testimony to continental drift.

A rowan blazes with autumn colour against a background of lava, Þingvellir national park, southwest Iceland.

Hlíðarendi in Fljótshlíð, south Iceland. The saga hero Gunnar chose
to risk death rather than be exiled from this beautiful spot.

Mýrdalsjökull, south Iceland: submerged beneath the ice-cap is the
volcano Katla, the origin of frequent earth tremors and floods.

Clouds collect on Mt. Vörðufell, close to Hestfjall, the epicentre of earthquake activity in south Iceland.

Above: Sea-eroded lava forms a gallery of bizarre shapes
at Arnarstapi on the Snæfellsnes peninsula, west Iceland.

Right: Kittiwakes nesting on the cliffs at Arnarstapi, with the
village and the pyramidal form of Mt. Stapafell beyond.

Cliffs rising to 534 m at Hornbjarg provide nesting ledges for one of Iceland's biggest colonies of seabirds, Hornstrandir region, northwest Iceland.

Moss and bog cotton brighten the harsh terrain on the footpath between Hornvík and Látravík, Hornstrandir region, northwest Iceland.

Rauðisandur (Red Sand) in the West Fjords, now the haunt of seals, was once home to a flourishing farming community.

The last in a long line of churches at Selárdalur, dating from 1861:
the parish was moved to a new location in 1907, West Fjords.

Not far off, the Fjallfoss falls, also known as Dynjandi, cascade
down a 100-m series of rock strata into Arnarfjörður fjord.

The deserted Hornvík bay once supported three farms and a harbour, Hornstrandir region, northwest Iceland.

Dyrhólaey in south Iceland. The headland, with its distinctive
arch, is renowned for its puffin colony.

Unlike the black volcanic sands of the south, Rauðisandur's
golden sweep is made up of crushed shells, West Fjords.

The bird cliffs of Hælavíkurbjarg (258 m), seen from the ascent of Hornbjarg, Hornstrandir region, northwest Iceland.

View from the Hornbjarg cliffs: fog and drizzle often testify to the proximity of drift ice,
Hornstrandir region, northwest Iceland.

Above: Barnafoss (Children's Falls), in the Hvítá river, is said to be
named after two boys who drowned there, Borgarfjörður district, west Iceland.

Right: Further down the same river, water gushes from the lava
over a kilometre-long stretch, creating the unusual Hraunfossar (Lava Falls).

A bonfire celebrates the light midsummer night at Ófeigsfjörður, in the remote Strandir region, northwest Iceland.

Mountain bikers traverse the demanding Kjölur
route across the west-central highlands.

Enjoying the hot springs at Hveravellir, deep in
the interior, on the Kjölur highland route.

Above: The geyser Strokkur spouts every few minutes to
the delight of onlookers at Geysir, southwest Iceland.

Right: Bláhver (Blue Spring) is one of the many hot springs
at Hveravellir on the Kjölur route, west-central highlands.

Langisjór (Long Lake), in the south-central highlands, is so remote that the first recorded sighting of it was not until the mid-19th century.

Brattháls, near Lake Álftavatn in the south-central highlands:
the Landmannalaugar-Þórsmörk hiking trail passes nearby.

From the Fögrufjöll range, looking along Lake Langisjór
to the Vatnajökull ice-cap, south-central highlands.

Above: Arctic riverbeauty (*Epilobium latifolium*), a North American
species found nowhere else in Europe, eastern highlands.

Right: The colourful and dramatic landscape of the
Kerlingarfjöll mountains in the west-central highlands.

View over the rhyolite ridges surrounding Landmannalaugar, taken from Mt. Bláhnúkur, south-central highlands.

A scarlet splash of iron deposits gives its name to Rauðfossar
(Red Falls) in the Rauðfossafjöll range, south-central highlands.

At nearby Landmannalaugar, the dark knobbly forms
of obsidian lava flows contrast with colourful rhyolite deposits.

Early autumn snows streak the moss on Stóra Súla, Landmannalaugar-Þórsmörk hiking trail, south-central highlands.

Steam hisses from a vent southwest of Hrafntinnusker,
on the Landmannalaugar-Þórsmörk hiking trail.

The spectacular rhyolite ravine at Brandsgil,
near Landmannalaugar, south-central highlands.

Ljótipollur, the inappropriately named "Ugly Pool", near Landmannalaugar, south-central highlands.

Glacial silt gives this oxbow lake by the river Tungnaá its milky-green tinge, south-central highlands.

Above: Veiðivötn (Fishing Lakes), a 20-km-long series
of water-filled craters in the south-central highlands.

Right: The Litla-Fossvatn rapids connect two of the lakes.
There are thought to be around 50 in all.

Moss softens the tephra landscape of the Veiðivötn crater lakes, south-central highlands.

Mt. Þóristindur, in the south-central highlands, is veiled by a sandstorm, a common hazard in Iceland's black deserts.

Reykjadalir (Smoky Valleys), a high-temperature zone reeking
with fumaroles and mud springs, south-central highlands.

Nearby, geothermal steam has hollowed out caves in the ice
at Hrafntinnusker, close to the Torfajökull glacier.

Landmannalaugar from Mt. Bláhnúkur, with the Laugahraun lava flow to the left
and the campsite beyond, south-central highlands.

Moss-cloaked lava near Hólaskjól, on the northern "Behind the Mountains" route, south-central highlands.

Goðafoss, named for the statues of pagan gods thrown into the falls
after Iceland's conversion to Christianity in 1000 AD, northeast Iceland.

Ásbyrgi canyon, fabled to be the hoofprint of Óðin's eight-legged steed
Sleipnir, was in fact created by a massive glacial flood, northeast Iceland.

Birch woods at Höfði on Lake Mývatn, northeast Iceland.
This lush vegetation provides a marked contrast to the lake's lunar surroundings.

The late Sigurveig Sigtryggsdóttir in her kitchen at the farm
of Syðri Neslönd, Lake Mývatn, northeast Iceland.

Jón í Belg fishing for trout through a hole in the ice: the shallow
waters of Lake Mývatn freeze for six months of the year.

Steam rises from the biggest concentration of mud springs
in the country at Hverarönd, Mývatn area, northeast Iceland.

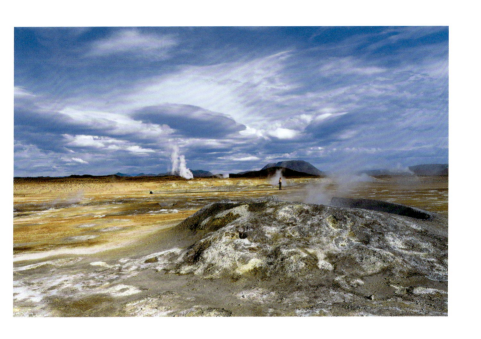

High temperatures lurk under the thin crust at Hverarönd
and sightseers are advised to watch their step.

113

Above: Climbing Mt. Námafjall (Mine Mountain),
named for the sulphur mines once located in its flanks.

Right: Sulphur and gypsum deposits lend the earth its brilliant
hue at Námaskarð, Mývatn area, northeast Iceland.

Deposits from mud springs have created wide clay pans at Hverarönd, Mývatn area, northeast Iceland.

View from Námafjall of Mt. Bláfjall, formed by a subglacial eruption during the last Ice Age, Mývatn area, northeast Iceland.

The most recent eruption at Leirhnjúkur began in 1975 and continued, with intervals, until 1984, Mývatn area, northeast Iceland.

Ódáðahraun, a vast lava field in the central highlands,
provides some of the bleakest scenery in the country.

Herðubreið (1,682 m), known as the "Queen of Mountains"
for its beautiful form, towers over the eastern highlands.

Mountain hut at Herðubreiðarlindir, an oasis of streams and vegetation near
Mt. Herðubreið in the desolate eastern highlands.

Rauðhólar are the cores of old craters swept away by a
catastrophic flood in the Jökulsá á Fjöllum river.

Basalt columns form a natural "elf-church" in the
Jökulsárgljúfur canyon, northeastern highlands.

Dettifoss is Europe's most powerful waterfall, with a flow of 500 m³ per second,
Jökulsárgljúfur canyon, northeastern highlands.

A sandwiched layer of basalt columns at Aldeyjarfoss falls in the Skjálfandafljót river, northeast Iceland.

Above: The gannet is the largest seabird in the North Atlantic: more than 10% of the world population nests in Iceland.

Right: Gannets breed on isolated islands and sea stacks, such as here at Karl off the Langanes peninsula, northeast Iceland.

The late Ásgeir Emilsson with his lively mural depicting Seyðisfjörður's dependence on the sea, east Iceland.

Kittiwakes swarm along the shore of Skoruvík cove on the
uninhabited Langanes peninsula, northeast Iceland.

Shorn-off ends of basalt columns in the Hljóðaklettar
cliffs, Vesturdalur valley, northeastern highlands.

Iron desposits create a startling burst of colour in the Markarfljótsgljúfur gorge, south-central highlands.

Curved basalt columns resemble organ pipes at Litlanesfoss falls in the Hengifossá river, east Iceland.

"Some people claim that in the silence of Iceland's wilderness, you come closest to hearing God."

ICELAND'S REGIONS

Southeast Iceland

Southeast Iceland is dominated by the 8,400 km^2 expanse of Vatnajökull, Europe's largest ice-cap. Not surprisingly, the landscape has been largely shaped by glaciation, with rugged, ice-scoured mountains around the rim of the glacier and vast outwash sands, braided with muddy glacial rivers, to the south. The sparse human population clings to the narrow coastal strip in isolated farms, with no towns or even villages between Kirkjubæjarklaustur to the west and Höfn í Hornafirði to the east. The ice-cap is ever present, looming as a white line on the horizon or descending in a series of picturesque glacial tongues, most spectacularly at Jökulsárlón (pp 22–23), where the Breiðamerkurjökull tongue has receded since 1950 to reveal a 100-m-deep lagoon, filled with icebergs calved from the glacier.

The flat, largely barren, sand plains (*sandur*) between the glacier and the sea are characterized by fast-flowing, capricious streams, whose frequent violent floods, or *jökulhlaup*, and changes of course formed a natural barrier to road-building until the final river was bridged in 1974. The power of these rivers was illustrated in dramatic fashion in 1996, when a volcanic eruption beneath Vatnajökull released millions of tons of meltwater and debris into the Skeiðará river, leaving colossal icebergs stranded on the sands and washing away both Ring Road and bridges to the south (pp 26–27).

Those living in the lee of the glacier know to their cost what a perilous neighbour it can be, despite the income it generates from tourism. Skaftafell National Park and nearby Svínafell (pp 16–17), at the foot of Iceland's highest peak, Hvannadalshnjúkur (2,110 m), enjoy a mild climate for much of the time, which encourages the growth of luxuriant birch forest and acts as a draw for walkers and campers. But a lone rowan tree, all that remains of the settlement at Sandfell, stands like a silent witness to the glacier's powers of destruction (pp 20–21). This once significant church and farm site was surrounded by violent flooding during the Öræfajökull eruptions of 1362 and 1727, when icebergs carried down by glacial meltwater remained stranded on the plain, in some cases for many years, before they thawed. Yet, in the end, it was economic factors that caused the last inhabitants to leave in 1947, part of a general trend towards depopulation of the countryside.

One building that has survived its proximity to the ice-cap is the attractive turf church at Hof (p. 19), the latest of its type to be built in Iceland (1883–5). This traditional construction style of dry-stone walls and a turf roof characterized buildings in Iceland until it was replaced by timber and latterly concrete in the 20th century.

With no natural harbours nearer than Höfn, people living in the shadow of the ice-cap have generally made their living by agriculture. Evidence of folk tradition associated with farming is found in the unusual place-names at Baulutjörn and Fláajökull, which translate as "Roaring Pond" and "Flaying Glacier" respectively (pp 28–29). According to legend, a bull was once slaughtered at the farm of Holt. When the men were halfway through flaying the carcass they were called in to eat. Meanwhile, a small bird flew down the bull's throat and the carcass began to stir. The men emerged to see the half-flayed bull plunge into a nearby pond. Since that time, it is said that the sound of a bull roaring periodically echoes from its waters and is believed to be a harbinger of storms.

South Iceland

A wide swathe of fertile lowland makes the Suðurland district Iceland's main agricultural area. It is also one of the most visited regions in the country, thanks to the presence of the popular "Golden Circle" of tourist attractions on its borders.

Despite the gentle appearance of the landscape, the country's most volatile volcanic and earthquake belt runs straight through this region. To the northeast, the ominous bulk of Hekla (1,491 m), one of Iceland's most active volcanoes, broods over the grassy lowlands (p. 30). Believed in late medieval Europe to be the mouth of hell, Hekla has erupted at least 18 times since the settlement of Iceland. Signs of devastating past eruptions scar the landscape all around. The 1947 outburst lasted 13 months and covered a 10 km^2 area with lava flows, though more recent activity, such as that in 2000, has been short-lived and "tourist friendly".

To the north are two of Iceland's most popular spectacles. Gullfoss (p. 15), arguably the most picturesque waterfall in the land, narrowly escaped being harnessed to power a hydroelectric plant in the early 20th century, being saved for posterity only by the courageous stance of a local landowner's daughter, Sigríður Tómasdóttir. Just down the road, Strokkur (p. 74), the most active spouting spring at the Geysir site, shoots up a plume of hot water and steam every few minutes to the delight of tourists. Its larger neighbour Geysir, from which the word "geyser" is derived, was largely dormant until revived by earthquakes in the year 2000.

Third of the trio of most-visited sites is Þingvellir (pp 40–45), the "Parliament Plains". It was here in this dramatic rift valley that the early settlers founded the Althing, often referred to as the world's oldest parliament, in 930 AD. The Althing is now held in Reykjavík but Þingvellir still attracts hundreds of thousands of visitors every year, for its interest is not solely historical; it also provides a vivid reminder that Iceland is located on the Mid-Atlantic Ridge, at the meeting point between the North American and Eurasian continental plates. Deep chasms, and the wide depression containing Iceland's largest natural lake, demonstrate clearly how the land is slowly tearing apart and growing, though the main fault line has now shifted southeast. Today, seismic activity in the region centres around

Mt. Hestfjall, the origin of two earthquakes measuring 6.5 on the Richter scale in June 2000.

As elsewhere in Iceland, farming in Suðurland consists mainly of animal husbandry, including dairy and beef farming, and grass cultivation, though greenhouses heated by geothermal power provide more exotic crops, from tomatoes to bananas, at places such as Hveragerði and Flúðir. Sheep farming is also characteristic of the region, and despite a recent drastic reduction of stock, sheep still outnumber Iceland's human population by two to one. From mid May to early June, the ewes drop their lambs (p. 34) and are sheared (p. 35), before being released to run wild in the mountains over the summer. In September, farmers head out, on foot or horseback in the roughest terrain, to round up their flocks (p. 36). The sheep spend the long winter in barns, feeding on hay.

The Mýrdalsjökull ice-cap (pp 32–33), like its larger cousin Vatnajökull, has had a profound effect on the surrounding landscape; the subglacial volcano Katla causes frequent minor earthquakes and floods in the rivers that flow across the 700 km^2 black waste of Mýrdalssandur to the southeast.

At the southernmost point in the land, the distinctive sea arch and stacks of the Dyrhólaey headland (p. 62), home to countless puffins and other seabirds, rise from the otherwise featureless sands of the coast. If sand and gravel continue to accumulate at the current rate, Dyrhólaey could be landlocked in a few hundred years.

West Iceland

The west of Iceland is best known for its three peninsulas: the lava-covered Reykjanes, the long mountainous spine of Snæfellsnes, capped by the famous Snæfellsjökull glacier, and the jagged protuberance of the West Fjords. Inland, the gentle, scrub-grown landscape of Borgarfjörður features attractive waterfalls among old lava fields (pp 68–69).

Lava has created bizarre formations along the coastline at Arnarstapi (pp 50–51), a fishing village on the south coast of Snæfellsnes, where the harbour bristles with rock pillars, eroded by the surf into distinctive shapes and white with the droppings of seabirds, such as kittiwake and fulmar.

A very different landscape takes over in the West Fjords, where great block-like mountains, indented with fjords, show classic signs of glaciation. Most remote of all, the uninhabited Hornstrandir region juts northwest into the Arctic Ocean. Once dotted with farms and fishing harbours, the lonely peninsula is now a nature reserve. Although the climate here is among the harshest in Iceland, with long winters and heavy snowfall, lush vegetation thrives in low-lying areas such as Hornvík bay (pp 60–61), thanks largely to the absence of sheep from the reserve. This natural harbour long provided shelter for storm-driven ships and its grassy lowlands once supported three farms. Now it is the domain of seabirds and Arctic foxes, accessible only in summer by boat from Ísafjörður or on foot via a long hiking trail. Driftwood from as far away as Siberia lines its beaches, a source of valuable building material in times gone by.

Hornvík lies between the great birdcliffs of Hornbjarg (pp 52–53) and Hælavíkurbjarg (pp 64–65). Made up of regular layers of basalt lavas and softer, sedimentary rock, these cliffs contain some of the oldest rocks in the country and the remains of fossilized trees have been found deep in their strata. Hornbjarg is home to the largest seabird colony in Iceland, with razorbills, guillemots, puffins, fulmars and kittiwakes numbering in their millions. In former times the human inhabitants of Hornstrandir supplemented their income by lowering themselves on ropes over these hair-raising precipices to collect birds and eggs. Although the last farmers abandoned their harsh life in this region in 1952, their descendants and other visitors still return during the summer to enjoy the solitude and astounding beauty. A popular walking trail connects the bays of Hornvík and Látravík (pp 54–55), but away from the sheltered coves with their banks of wildflowers, the terrain is forbidding, the kingdom of mosses and lichens. Even in summer, the Greenland sea ice often drifts close to the coast, bringing fog, cold drizzle and snow.

Further south in the West Fjords, the climate is marginally milder and the population still clings on, concentrated in a series of fishing villages in the western fjords. Isolated farms and settlements have largely been forsaken as untenable. This was the fate of Selárdalur (p. 58), where the church stands as an evocative reminder of earlier times when it was an important parish centre and the seat of influential priests.

On the southern shore of the West Fjords, bordering Breiðafjörður bay, the climate can seem almost kind, and the golden sweep of Rauðisandur (pp 56–57) gives a misleading impression of Mediterranean warmth. This picturesque place, now largely the haunt of seals, once supported a flourishing farming community, and two families still make a living from its cultivable fringe of lowland. In the 19th century, Sjöundá in Rauðisandur was the atmospheric setting for a true story of passion and murder, later celebrated in the novel *Svartfugl* (lit. Black Bird) by Gunnar Gunnarsson. In 1802, the lovers Bjarni Bjarnason and Steinunn Sigurðardóttir, who lived on neighbouring farms, murdered their respective spouses and were condemned to death for their crimes.

The Interior

While the human population lives in sparse settlements around the coast or crowded into the southwestern corner of Iceland, most of the country is uninhabited and uninhabitable wilderness.

A vast, treeless wasteland of sand desert, lava, rock and ice, like nothing found elsewhere in Europe, it is accessible only to 4WD vehicles, and even then only during the summer months of July and August.

In past centuries, the Icelanders would traverse the interior with trains of packhorses to trade or attend the Althing at Þingvellir, and cairn-marked trails still criss-cross the empty landscape. Drovers in search of sheep were the only other people who regularly ventured into the highlands, which were rumoured to be the haunt of dangerous outlaws and supernatural terrors, such as elves and trolls.

The mountain route over Kjölur (p. 72), which crosses the interior between the Langjökull and Hofsjökull ice-caps, follows the course of one of these ancient packhorse trails. The unmetalled road starts in the south just beyond Geysir and Gullfoss, and passes north over a stony, largely featureless plateau, with long views to the white ice-caps on either side. About halfway, however, the traveller is rewarded by the geothermal area at Hveravellir where one can bathe in the naturally heated waters or wander among mud pools and steaming springs (p. 73).

For the most varied scenery in the interior, however, nothing compares with the south-central highlands. Here volcanic activity has produced a very different effect to the forbidding terrain of much of the centre. An eruption in 1477 led to the production of black rhyolitic lavas, contrasting with the area's subglacially formed rhyolitic rocks which seem to come in every colour of the rainbow and are particularly striking around the Landmannalaugar hot springs (pp 82–83). Here a campsite and mountain hut provide a base for exploring the region, and a starting point for the well-trodden "Laugavegur" hiking trail to Þórsmörk. Dark, obsidian-coated lava from the Laugahraun flow makes a startling contrast to the brilliant rhyolite (p. 85), while an oasis of grass and flowering plants clusters around the hot bathing pool, despite the 600-m altitude of the site. In this youthful landscape of fantastic geological forms, steam rises from innumerable vents, and in the high-temperature zone concentrated around the small Torfajökull glacier to the south, steam action has hollowed out deep caverns in the ice (p. 101). Two mountain roads, the north and south "Behind the Mountains" routes, penetrate this region, carrying the traveller past mossy peaks, red rocks and black sands (pp 86–87). Anglers brave these rough tracks in summer to visit Veiðivötn (pp 94–97), a series of crater lakes in the south of the region, which provide good fishing for trout. The craters were formed in 1477, during the same cataclysm that led to the creation of the Landmannalaugar area.

To the east, and accessible only to the hardiest vehicles, is the fjord-like expanse of Langisjór (pp 76–77), the "Long Lake", bordering on the Vatnajökull ice-cap. It is thought that no one laid eyes on Langisjór until 1878 when drovers seeking their flocks wandered further than usual into the interior. Here the landscape appears untouched by man, though plans to divert the Skaftá river for a hydroelectric scheme could change all that.

Northeast Iceland

The chief scenic wonders of northeast Iceland have been shaped by the forces of fire and water, more specifically volcanism and glacial floods. The single biggest attraction in the area is Mývatn (pp 108–9), literally "Midge Lake", with its unrivalled wealth of birdlife, particularly duck species, not to mention the scourge of its midges. The locals have practised farming since the earliest times, taking advantage of the abundant vegetation on the lake's shores, as well as the opportunities it offers for trout-fishing (p. 111) and egg collecting. During the 20th century, alternative industries emerged in the area, such as the controversial diatomite extraction plant set up in 1967 to profit from the lake's deep layer of diatoms, the geothermal power station at Krafla, and now tourism.

Mývatn's greatest attraction lies in its huge range of volcanic features, from pseudo-craters to lava sculptures, active volcanoes and boiling mud pools. It comes as no surprise that US astronauts rehearsed their 1969 moon landing in the lunar landscape to the south of the lake. In summer, visitors flock to see the sulphurous yellow soil and steaming solfataras at Hverarönd (pp 112–13), the biggest collection of mud springs in the country. Here the signs of volcanic activity spread out as far as the eye can see, steam churning out of vents with throat-tearing fumes, the ground so hot under its thin crust that sightseers must tread with care. For centuries the Danish kings mined sulphur from the hillside at Námaskarð (p. 116–17) to provide gunpowder for their continental wars.

Nearby, the highly active Krafla fissure has erupted at least 16 times since the settlement of the country (pp 120–21), most recently in 1984, and the geothermal power station now takes advantage of all this natural energy to provide electricity for the towns of north Iceland. In the distance loom great, flat-topped mountains such as Búrfell and Herðubreið (p. 123), the "Queen of Mountains", created by lava welling up and spreading out under the ice-sheets during Ice Ages past. To the south, the dark sand desert of Ódáðahraun (p. 122) must surely be one of the most desolate, yet awe-inspiring, places in the country.

The ability of water to sculpt the landscape is graphically illustrated by the mud-coloured cataract of Dettifoss (pp 128–29), the most powerful waterfall in Europe. Dettifoss is just one of a series of spectacular cascades in the Jökulsá á Fjöllum river, a debris-laden glacial torrent which rises under the Vatnajökull ice-cap and cuts its way north through the highland plateau all the way to the sea. Volcanic activity caused the subglacial lake under Vatnajökull to empty in its entirety 10,000 and again 3,000 years ago, resulting in gigantic floods which moulded many of the breathtaking features visible today. A wall of water is believed to have gouged out the stupendous 30 km trough of the Jökulsárgljúfur canyon in one fell swoop, while the horseshoe-shaped canyon at Ásbyrgi (p. 107), now filled with birch and rowan, was originally carved out by a waterfall.

Sometimes referred to as Iceland's Grand Canyon, Jökulsárgljúfur is a gallery of extraordinary geological sculptures, from the unbelievable red of the Rauðhólar (p. 126), with their eroded rock pinnacles, to the myriad formations of basalt pillars and columns. It is hard to believe that the "elf church" (p. 127) at Hafragilsundirlendi is not the work of man – or supernatural beings. In other places in the rivers of the north and east, basalt columns recall organ pipes (pp 140–41) or the architecture of a gothic cathedral (pp 6–7), more imposing by far than the simple lineaments of an Icelandic country church (p. 142).

Last outpost to the northeast is the lonely Langanes peninsula, populated solely by birds, where gannets, the kings of the North Atlantic, crowd the sheer rock Karl (pp 132–33) on the edge of the Arctic Ocean.

FACTS ABOUT ICELAND

Geography

Located just south of the Arctic Circle, Iceland is Europe's second-largest island at 103,000 km^2 and one of the youngest countries in the world in geological terms. Sitting astride the Mid-Atlantic Ridge, on the fault-line between the North American and Eurasian continental plates, the island is still in the process of being formed. No rocks over 20 million years old have been found on land and much of the country seems to have grown up only during the last million years or so. The newest offshore island, Surtsey, emerged from the sea in an eruption as recently as 1963.

Volcanoes

As a result of its location, Iceland is one of the most volcanically active countries in the world. Around 20 volcanic systems are active today, and there have been more than 250 recorded eruptions since the settlement of the island in the late ninth century. Most common are fissure eruptions, though almost every type of volcano is found in the country, the most active volcanic systems being those of Hekla, Katla, Grímsvötn and the Westman Islands in the south, and Askja and Krafla in the north. The most destructive eruption on record is that of Laki in 1783, during which airborne ash and gaseous substances created a "nuclear winter" effect, wiping out one-fifth of the population and half the country's domestic livestoc. Today 11% of the landscape is covered by lava fields.

Earthquakes

These are common but rarely harmful, as modern Icelandic buildings are built to withstand all but the strongest tremors. Nevertheless, in 2000 and 2008 earthquakes measuring 6.3-6.5 on the Richter scale destroyed dozens of buildings in the southwest.

Geothermal heat

There is more high-temperature and geothermal activity in Iceland than in any other country in the world. The largest of the 32 high-temperature zones are Torfajökull and Grímsvötn in the south, while Hengill, near Reykjavík, provides hot water for domestic heating in the capital. There are around 250 low-temperature fields, found almost everywhere except the far east of the country. The average temperature of the water is 75°C/167°F. Geysers are found in a number of areas, the most active being Strokkur at the Geysir site, which erupts every few minutes.

Glaciers

The name Iceland is something of a misnomer as only 11.6% of country is actually covered in ice. The largest ice-cap is Vatnajökull at 8,400 km^2, with an ice-depth of up to 1 km at its thickest. The other major ice-caps are Langjökull 950 km^2, Hofsjökull 925 km^2 and Mýrdalsjökull 595 km^2. All these glaciers are remnants of the last Ice Age and are gradually retreating as the climate grows warmer.

Climate

This varies between Arctic in the north and oceanic cool-temperate in the south, with temperatures relatively mild due to the influence of the Gulf Stream. The mean temperature in Reykjavík in summer is 10.5°C/51°F and in winter -0.5°C/31.1°F. Weather tends to be highly unpredictable and strong winds are common.

Midnight Sun

Iceland's northerly position results in short, dark winter days and long, bright summer nights. In midwinter the sun creeps above the horizon for only four hours a day in Reykjavík, while in midsummer it is visible for over 22 hours a day and the sky remains light all night. However, the true midnight sun can only be seen from the north coast of the country.

Flora and Fauna

Iceland's ecosystem is characterized by a paucity of species, a result of the island's newness, isolated location and the fact that it has never been attached to the mainland. Prior to the arrival of man, only flora and fauna which could be borne on the wind or travel by sea were able to colonize the island.

Vegetation

Only about 23% of the land surface is covered with permanent vegetation. This is due to the harsh climate, volcanic activity, glacier movements and, not least, soil erosion caused by centuries of overgrazing and deforestation. It is thought that more than half the plant cover has been lost since the settlement, when birch forest was reported to clothe the land between the mountains and the sea. Only around 520 species of flowering plants are found in Iceland, the most common being low-lying shrubs of a sub-arctic character, such as heather, berries, willow and dwarf birch. Lower plants such as mosses and lichens are more abundant.

Wildlife

Iceland's fauna is dominated by birds, with 75 species of breeding birds and large numbers of migrants. The largest groups are seabirds, waterfowl and waders. Birds make up in sheer quantity what they lack in variety. The puffin, one of the most common species, has an estimated population of 10 million. Other fauna is extremely limited. The only native mammal is the Arctic fox, though the seas around Iceland are populated by common and grey seals, and 12 species of whale, including the giant blue whale. Most land species have been introduced by man, including domestic animals such as sheep, horses, cows, pigs and reindeer, and inadvertently introduced species such as rats, mice and mink. Freshwater fish abound in the rivers but are limited to species such as salmon, trout and Arctic charr. Iceland is unusual in having no amphibians or reptiles.

People

Iceland was settled by people of Norse and Celtic origin, the first colonizers arriving in the late ninth century from Scandinavia via the British Isles.

Language

Icelandic is a Nordic language that has changed little since medieval times. It is related to the Scandinavian languages but retains the old letters þ (like the "th" in "thing") and ð (like the "th" in "then"). Loanwords are avoided where possible and replaced by native creations, such as *sími* (telephone) and *þota* (jet). English is widely understood.

Names

Very few Icelanders have surnames. Most use a patronymic, formed from their father's name plus *"son"* for men and *"dóttir"* for women. People are listed under their first names in the telephone directory.

History

Iceland was the last European country to be settled. According to ancient records, the first permanent settler was Ingólfur Arnarson in 874 AD, who set up home on the site now occupied by Reykjavík. In 930, the settlers established a general assembly at Þingvellir, known as the Althing, to rule the country. Among the most famous achievements of the Althing was the peaceful conversion to Christianity in 1000. The so-called Commonwealth, a republic made up of 39 independent chieftaincies or *goðorð*, lasted till 1262 when the country came under Norwegian rule. In 1380 the Danish crown took over

Iceland and for more than 500 years the country remained a Danish territory. A growing independence movement in the 19th century led to the granting of a constitution in 1874 and culminated in the recognition of Iceland as a sovereign state under the Danish crown in 1918. The Second World War precipitated huge changes in Icelandic society when the country was occupied, first by British forces in 1940, then by the US in 1942, resulting in a new prosperity and accelerating the process of modernization. In 1944 the Icelanders declared their independence and the Republic of Iceland was inaugurated at Þingvellir on 17th June, now celebrated as Icelandic National Day.

Government

Today Iceland is a constitutional republic with a president and parliament, the Althing. All citizens receive the right to vote at 18, and parliamentary and presidential elections are held every four years.

Society

Iceland is a welfare state with free education and hospital care for all. The population is highly educated and enjoys one of the highest standards of living in the world.

Population

Iceland's population of only 320,000 makes it the most sparsely populated country in Europe, with a mere 3.1 people per km^2. Over the last 50 years, the country has gone from being an essentially rural society to an urban one, with only 8% of the inhabitants living in rural areas today. The world's northernmost capital, Reykjavík is a modern, bustling city with a lively cultural and nightlife. Some 60% per cent of the population, or 200,000 people, now live in the capital area. The largest town outside the southwest is Akureyri in north Iceland with 18,000 inhabitants.

Economy

Iceland has limited natural resources, and so Icelanders are heavily dependent on foreign trade. A large range of commodities are imported, while there is little diversity in exports.

Rich fishing grounds around Iceland have long been the mainstay of the economy, and the principal source of export revenues; until recent years economic fluctuations have been almost entirely a function of catches and their value on foreign markets. As recently as the turn of the 21st century fish products accounted for two-thirds of export revenues, but this proportion has fallen in the past decade.

Geothermal and water power have gradually acquired importance; natural hot water is used for heating, and rivers have been harnessed to generate electricity for Icelandic homes. Today this relatively "green" energy is increasingly being used for industrial purposes. Industry has become one of Iceland's major economic sectors – not least energy-intensive metals industry – and today more than half of export revenue derives from industrial production.

Agricultural products yield only a tiny fraction of export revenues, but the agricultural sector supplies almost all Iceland's meat and dairy products; and vegetable crops are cultivated in some quantity, including horticulture in greenhouses with geothermal heating.

In the early 2000s the financial sector appeared to be booming and Icelandic banks expanded rapidly, but that period came to an end in 2008 with the collapse of the banks and the economy, and since then Iceland has been making a gradual recovery. Information technology and various creative sectors are flourishing, while the biggest growth area is tourism, with unprecedented numbers of visitors to Iceland; the economic and natural shocks experienced by Iceland in recent years appear to have made it a place of interest internationally.

Culture

Iceland enjoys a thriving arts scene, its literature, music and film-making in particular gaining recognition abroad in recent years. Undoubtedly the most famous Icelander in the world today is the singer Björk, and the country has become known as an exporter of pop talent. However, Iceland's greatest contribution to European culture are the Family Sagas, prose novels written during the 12th and 13th centuries, recounting the exploits of the early Icelandic settlers. Best-known are *Njál's Saga, Egil's Saga* and *Laxdæla Saga*, which have been translated into numerous languages. The Eddic poems, composed between 800 and 1200, are considered among the great heroic and mythological epics of world literature, and provided source material for Wagner's Ring cycle. Manuscripts of the Sagas and Eddic poems, the majority of which have been returned to the country since 1971 by the Danes, are regarded as the nation's greatest treasure. And books continue to be regarded highly in Iceland. Much is made of the fact that the author Halldór Laxness won the Nobel Prize for Literature in 1955, and more titles are published per capita in Iceland than anywhere else in the world.